IN GOD'S COMPANY
Christian Giants of Business

by Peter Lupson

THOMAS COOK
TRAVEL PIONEER

There is no name in the world more immediately recognisable in connection with travel than **Thomas Cook**, the founder of a business empire worth billions. Yet the furthermost thought from Thomas Cook's mind when he organised his first ever railway excursion was making money. Throughout his career as a tour organiser his sense of service to others was paramount. His life's mission and greatest passion was to bring *"man nearer to man and nearer to his Creator"* by making travel affordable and accessible to all.

Painful early years

Above: Boulder and plaque marking birthplace

Nothing in Thomas's early life remotely suggested it would lead to him becoming a household name across the globe. Born at 9 Quick Close, Melbourne, Derbyshire, on 22 November 1808, he was the son of a labourer, John Cook, who died in 1812 when Thomas was only three. Later that year his mother Elizabeth married James Smithard, also a labourer, and had two sons with him, James and Simeon.

Above: The view towards Melbourne Parish Church

The early years of his life in Melbourne were marked by considerable pain and hardship. Money was so tight in the household that Thomas had to leave school at the age of ten to supplement the family income. He was employed by John Roby, a market gardener and a heavy drinker. His first job assisting

Roby was in the gardens of Melbourne Hall. The work was physically demanding. It involved fetching and carrying heavy sacks and baskets and a considerable amount of digging.

Above: Melbourne Hall

Roby's addiction to alcohol put extra strain on Thomas. Roby was often the worse for wear after a drinking bout and incapable of selling the estate's garden produce in the neighbouring villages. It was left to Thomas to take on this extra work.

In 1820 Thomas had an even greater burden to bear when his kind and supportive stepfather, James Smithard, died. It was the second time in his childhood that he had lost a father. Immediately after Smithard's burial, he was told by his mother: *"Now, Tommy, you must be father to these two boys."* A very heavy responsibility indeed for a 12-year-old.

Sadly, his struggles seemed never-ending. Two years later he began a five-year apprenticeship as a wood-turner and cabinet-maker with his uncle, John Pegg. But Pegg, like Roby, was an alcoholic and once again Thomas found himself burdened with an increased workload because of drink. He later recalled:

> *"The turner sought his relaxation and enjoyment night after night in a snug corner in the village public-house, where much of his time was wasted and his means so dissipated that, notwithstanding a good business, he lived and died a poor man."*

Witnessing the damaging effects of drink at close quarters over long periods scarred Thomas but, as we shall see, these disturbing experiences were to prove blessings in disguise. They led to his active involvement in the Temperance Movement, the fight against drink and the misery it caused, and this, in turn, became the springboard for his amazing career in the travel business.

"The earnest, active, devoted, young Christian"
It was during those years of struggle in his adolescence that the seeds of Thomas's deep Christian faith were sown. Through his

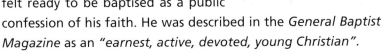

Right: Melbourne Baptist Chapel

Inset: Joseph Winks

faith he found the strength to persevere. At the age of 14 he began to attend the Sunday school of Melbourne Baptist Chapel and showed such commitment that he was promoted first to teacher, then superintendent. At the age of 17, he felt ready to be baptised as a public confession of his faith. He was described in the *General Baptist Magazine* as an *"earnest, active, devoted, young Christian"*.

The minister of Melbourne Baptist Chapel, Joseph Winks, had a profound guiding influence on Thomas who looked up to him as a father, and through whom his *"soul was won for Christ."*. He had launched the *Baptist Children's Magazine* in 1825 and had set up a printing press in Loughborough. He tried to combine his publishing activities with his ministry in Melbourne but found it impossible. He therefore left Melbourne in 1826 to devote himself to publishing magazines *"for the young and the poor"*.

When Pegg's drinking became too much for Thomas he gave up his apprenticeship aged 18 to join Winks in Loughborough to learn the art of printing and publishing.

The call to evangelism
During his time in Loughborough, Thomas had become increasingly aware of the call to preach the Gospel, the good

5

news of God's gift of eternal life through Jesus Christ, His son. And so, aged 19, with the full backing of Melbourne Baptist Chapel, he successfully applied to the General Baptist Missionary Society to become an evangelist. He was entrusted with the duties of *"village missionary, tract distributor, and Sunday school promoter"* to serve in a number of localities in the Midlands.

The work of an itinerant evangelist was demanding. It required wholehearted devotion, unfailing energy and unflagging perseverance in the face of fierce opposition. There was no financial incentive to accept the calling. Thomas's income was meagre and, as he couldn't afford stage coach travel, he had to walk incredibly long distances. In 1829 alone he covered more than 2,000 miles on foot.

He also met with ridicule and contempt. Despite his kindly manner and warm smile, his preaching style was forceful and direct and he pulled no punches in confronting immorality. As a result, stones and other objects were thrown at him and he was physically assaulted. But he took all this in his stride. His fearlessness and passion for his work made him more than a match for the hecklers whose hissing he laughingly dismissed as *"Gooseism and Snakeism"*.

Above: *Barrowden*

Marriage

Thomas served as an evangelist for three years but then the funds of the Baptist Missionary Society ran out. As he needed to make a living, he set up in business as a wood-turner in the village of Barrowden in Rutland. He was drawn there because of his affection for Marianne Mason, a farmer's daughter he'd met two years previously at the Baptist chapel in Barrowden while an evangelist. Marianne was a teacher at the Sunday School. She kept house for her widower father and looked after

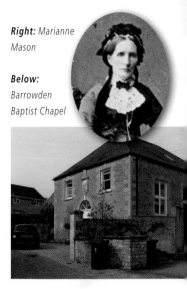

Right: Marianne Mason

Below: Barrowden Baptist Chapel

her 5 younger brothers. Thomas lodged with the family while he worked in the village.

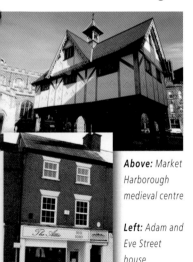

Above: Market Harborough medieval centre

Left: Adam and Eve Street house

However, there proved to be too little work for a wood-turner in Barrowden and so, in November 1832, Thomas relocated to Market Harborough with its larger population. He rented a house in Adam and Eve Street, and, just four months later, had earned enough to provide for a wife and family. He therefore proposed to Marianne and on 2 March 1833 they were married in St. Peter's Church in Barrowden. Thomas was

Above: *St. Peter's Church in Barrowden*

24, Marianne 26. Adam and Eve Street became their home for the next eight and a half years. Their first child, John Mason Cook, was born there in January 1834.

The energetic anti-drink campaigner

The move to Market Harborough on his own before his marriage had opened an important new chapter in Thomas's life. It was here that he became actively involved in the Temperance Movement, the crusade against drink, one of the biggest social problems of his day.

Pubs and so-called gin palaces offered a cheap and easily available form of escape from the mind-numbing conditions in which most workers lived. Their working hours were long and hard, their income was pitifully low and there were few, if any, home comforts. Families in towns lived in cramped, squalid conditions and there was little to cheer the spirit. To make matters worse, money that should have been spent on food and clothing was often squandered on drink. Alcohol-fuelled behaviour also became a problem in the streets where the sight of drunken brawls was all too common.

Not surprisingly, alcohol became the target of well-meaning social reformers. In 1832 Joseph Livesey founded the Preston Temperance Society which marked the birth of the Temperance Movement in England. The movement soon became associated in the public mind with the term 'teetotalism'. It was famously coined by one of Joseph Livesey's supporters, Richard Turner, a reformed alcoholic, when he defiantly stuttered:

"I'll have nowt to do with the moderation botheration pledge; I'll be reet down t-t-total, that or nowt."

Temperance campaigners formed national, regional and local societies open to any adult who signed a pledge to abstain from alcohol. They worked tirelessly to educate the public about the dangers of drink and created alcohol-free recreational facilities such as coffee houses, reading rooms, libraries, museums and parks as an alternative to pubs and gin palaces. They also arranged wholesome entertainment including concerts, singing, drama, readings and recitations.

Above: *Market Harborough Baptist Church*

9

Thomas's involvement with temperance began when he joined the Market Harborough Baptist Church of which the Revd Francis Beardsall, an agent of the British and Foreign Temperance Society, was minister. Beardsall's preaching against the dangers of drink struck a chord with him. He was only too well aware of these, having worked for two alcoholic employers. On New Year's day 1833 he responded to Revd Beardsall's appeal to

Above: Market Harborough Town Hall

sign the pledge agreeing *"to abstain from ardent spirits, and to discountenance the causes and practice of intemperance."*

The pledge at this stage applied only to spirits and Thomas, in fact, still kept beer and wine in his home. However, this changed early December 1836 when he heard a teetotal lecture in the Market Harborough Town Hall. It made such an impact on him that the next day he and six others formed the South Midland Temperance Association in the town. Thomas was appointed its secretary and from this time on he abstained from all forms of alcohol.

His commitment to the temperance cause was total. Fully supported by Marianne, he worked tirelessly as Secretary of the South Midland Temperance Association arranging meetings, attending conferences, organising bazaars, galas and other events. He also became a renowned public speaker. During his time as an evangelist he had developed considerable skill as a preacher and his ability to hold an audience without the use of notes once more came into its own.

Thomas also drew on another important experience from his past – printing and publishing. He threw himself wholeheartedly – entirely at his own expense – into producing a whole range of materials supporting the message of abstinence. It was a measure of his commitment that the sales of his publications barely covered costs. Furthermore, time spent printing was lost from wood-turning and so, inevitably, money was always tight.

Violent opposition

As Thomas had discovered in his time as an evangelist, not everyone wanted to hear his message. Once again he met with violent opposition, this time from brewers, publicans and their supporters. Fuelled by hatred, they hired thugs to attack temperance workers in the streets and damage their homes. Meetings in the Market Harborough town hall were almost always broken up. Thomas was booed, hissed and sneered at in the streets and stones were thrown at him. He vividly recalled the time:

"My house in Adam and Eve Street was violently assailed, and brick bats came flying through the window to the imminent danger of Mrs. Cook and myself. On one occasion a horse's leg bone taken from a cartload of bones was thrown at me with such violence that, striking me at the back of the neck, I was felled to the ground."

However, he was able to chase and catch his attacker and have him brought to court to face a hefty fine.

Above: *The Congregational Chapel in Kibworth Harcourt*

But far from weakening his resolve to fight against alcohol, ugly opposition merely served to strengthen it. It made him more determined than ever to find alternative forms of recreation to drink. Quite unexpectedly, on 9 June 1841, he hit on an idea that was to have far-reaching consequences ...

A ground-breaking idea

That day he set out from Market Harborough on a fifteen mile walk to Leicester to attend a quarterly meeting of temperance delegates. As he was passing the Congregational Chapel in Kibworth Harcourt, the recent extension of the railway network suddenly came into his mind and in a flash of inspiration he realised its possibilities. He recalled the moment many years later:

"From my residence at Market Harborough I walked to Leicester (15 miles) to attend that meeting. About midway between Harborough and Leicester – my mind's eye has often reverted to that spot – a thought flashed through my brain – what a glorious thing it would be if the newly-developed powers of railways and locomotion could be made subservient to the promotion of temperance!"

By the time he had reached the venue, the idea was fully formed. Addressing the delegates, he proposed that their next quarterly meeting in Loughborough should be turned into a special event on a non-profit basis. His plan was to charter a train as cheaply as possible from Leicester to Loughborough and back and arrange a fun day out for the public in a carnival atmosphere but with a series of temperance messages at the end. The response to his idea could not have been better:

> *"The Chairman approved, the meeting roared with excitement, and early next day I proposed my grand scheme to John Fox Bell, the resident secretary of the Midland Counties Railway Company."*

Below: William Paget's private park in Loughborough

Bell was also fully supportive. He not only gave his approval but also made a donation towards the cost of the event.

Cook's first railway excursion

Thomas immediately began planning the excursion. He secured cheap railway fares and made arrangements with a keen temperance supporter, William Paget, to hold a gala in his private park in Loughborough. He then advertised the event.

His hard work paid off. On Monday 5 July 1841, 500 passengers assembled at Leicester's Campbell Street Station to embark on their ten-mile journey. Never before had such a large number

travelled on a train. Such was the novelty of the occasion that over 2,000 people turned up at the station to witness their departure. A brass band added to the colour of the occasion.

Despite all the excitement some of the passengers were nervous of travelling by rail for the first time. And with good reason. 9 of the 10 carriages had no seats and no roofs and they accommodated as many people as could be squeezed in. There was no protection from rain, smoke, soot or sparks.

Thomas felt it essential, therefore, to escort the party personally to give them reassurance. He was always concerned for the comfort, safety and well-being of his clients and wanted to share with them not only the pleasures of travel but also the difficulties and hardships. This became a feature of all his pioneering excursions.

There was huge public interest in the event. Thomas wrote:

> *"People crowded the streets, filled windows, covered the house-tops, and cheered us all along the line with the heartiest welcome."*

14

The *Leicester Chronicle* reported that *"every bridge along the line was crowded to have a peep at the train in progress"*.

The train's arrival at Loughborough station met with unbelievable excitement from some 2,000 people who had gathered to welcome the excursionists. The carnival atmosphere began immediately as the intrepid passengers were led by a brass band from the station to William Paget's park.

There they were joined by local people and others who had travelled from nearby Midland towns.

In total some 3,000 people participated in the gala. They presented a colourful spectacle with many carrying flags and banners and decked out in temperance rosettes, ribbons and medals. The afternoon was spent in a whole range of leisure activities including cricket, dancing and games such as blind man's bluff and tag. It was a measure of Thomas's organisational skills that he provided a substantial picnic for all 3,000 at lunchtime and tea time.

The serious part of the day began at 6 p.m. For the next three hours the crowd listened to a series of rousing speeches by church ministers warning their listeners of the dangers of drink. Today this would seem a most unusual way of rounding off a day of fun and frivolity but at the time gifted public speakers who could hold an audience spellbound were often seen as an exciting form of entertainment.

When the event drew to a close, Thomas's party made their

way back to Loughborough Station for the return journey to Leicester. On arrival in Leicester at 10.30 p.m. they were enthusiastically welcomed by a huge crowd impressed by their pioneering spirit. The expedition had clearly been a massive success and had captured the public's imagination nationwide.

It's difficult for us to understand today why this ten-mile railway excursion should create so much excitement and become the focus of national interest. Perhaps if we imagine the likely reaction when the first large-scale tourist trip into outer space takes place, we might get some idea of how Thomas's achievement appeared in the eyes of his contemporaries. He himself recognised the significance of the event and always looked back on it as the birth of his career in the travel business.

Struggling printing business in Leicester

The success of the Loughborough excursion fired Thomas's imagination and inspired him to want to organise more in the

Above: *Town Hall Square, Leicester*

cause of temperance. He felt it would make sound practical sense to move to Leicester with its good rail connections in pursuit of this aim. He also saw the possibility of earning a better living there by setting up in business as a printer and publisher. And so, two months after the Loughborough trip, Thomas set up his new home and printing business at 1 King Street producing temperance literature and Baptist devotional works.

But his energies were not limited to printing and publishing. In 1843 he opened a temperance hotel (run by Marianne) at 28 Granby Street, Leicester, which served as the family home and his business HQ. He also continued his tireless work as secretary of the South Midland Temperance Association.

However, despite vigorously promoting his products, his business struggled, not least because he continually subsidised his unprofitable temperance publications. Although he ran a number of sidelines such as book-binding and the sale of stationery and pens, they did not cover his costs. In July 1843 he wrote that he had *"suffered great pecuniary losses and disappointments in his endeavours to serve the cause of true temperance"*.

Alongside his business activities, Thomas organised several cheap excursions to temperance events for *"rational and exquisite enjoyment"*. But they brought no income, being run as a labour of love on a non-profit basis. As he later explained:

"The work was one of enthusiastic philanthropy bringing with it its own reward, for during that time I never dreamt of it as a source of pecuniary interest."

By 1844, no doubt because of his financial pressures and the birth of a baby due in June the following year (his daughter Annie), he began to turn his thoughts to the potential of commercial tourism as an additional source of income. Aware that he had established a reputation as an outstanding travel organiser, he clearly felt this was a realistic step to take.

First commercial excursion – Liverpool and North Wales

The first step was to select a destination for his first commercial excursion. He decided on a trip from Leicester to Liverpool, an attractive city with many grand buildings and the gateway to the New World. From Liverpool his party would proceed by steamer to North Wales to visit Caernarfon and its magnificent castle and then ascend the mountain path to the summit of Snowdon.

Thomas soon discovered that planning the journey was not straightforward. The train from Leicester to Liverpool ran on the

lines of three different railway companies, each issuing their own separate tickets, and his first task was to try to convince these companies to issue a single ticket valid across their lines. He successfully negotiated an agreement with them then tried out the route himself. When everything was in place, he produced the *Handbook of the trip to Liverpool* with the full itinerary and information about the sights to be visited.

Above: *Handbook of the trip to Liverpool*

Right: Liverpool skyline

Below right: Caernarfon Castle and Quay

With everything in place he set about advertising the trip. As the price was low the response was unbelievable. The 1,200 available tickets were quickly snapped up and such was the demand that many were re-sold at exorbitant prices.

The world's first commercial tourist excursion departed Leicester at 5 a.m on Monday 4 August 1845 with Thomas in accompaniment. After a short stay in Liverpool, 350 of the party continued by steamer to Caernarfon. Their arrival there caused a sensation. It was the largest group of tourists ever seen in this Welsh-speaking town. Fortunately someone was found who spoke enough English to act as their

guide. After the tour and a visit to the magnificent castle, the next objective was Snowdon, Thomas leading the party up the footpath to the summit.

Left: Snowdon summit

Such was the success of the excursion that the *Leicester Chronicle* enthused: *"a more agreeable, rational and delightful amusement it is difficult to conceive."* A fortnight later Thomas repeated it with a group of 800 and it was another huge success. Overjoyed by the winning formula he had discovered, he quickly saw its potential for further development and wrote in his diary:

"From the heights of Snowdon my thoughts took flight to Ben Lomond, and I determined to try to get to Scotland."

He clearly had the beautiful scenery of Loch Lomond in his mind and the appeal for tourists of sailing on its waters.

A dream realised

With Scotland now firmly in his sights, Thomas made two exploratory visits there to find the most practical route. This was essential as there was no rail link from England, and Scotland was unknown territory to almost all English people. He finally decided the best way would be by rail from Leicester to Fleetwood, from there by steamer to Ardrossan and then on to Glasgow and Edinburgh by rail. Edinburgh would serve as the base for excursions to locations of scenic or historic interest.

To keep the price as low as possible he had to convince the rail and steamship companies that it would be more profitable for them to transport large numbers of passengers at a reduced fare than a small number at the normal rate. He managed to agree terms with them and then compiled a *Handbook of a Trip to Scotland* with information for the excursionists. With everything in place he duly advertised the trip and on 25 June 1846 his party of 350 set off from Leicester Station.

At first, through no fault of Thomas's, everything went wrong. Stops had been arranged en route to Fleetwood for refreshments and the use of toilet facilities (there were none on trains at the time) but it didn't happen. The situation was made worse when it was discovered there were too few cabins on the steamer for everyone

Above: Exterior of the City Halls (right), Glasgow

Below: Princes Street, Edinburgh

and many passengers, including Thomas, had to spend the rain-lashed, windswept night on deck. There was to be a serious backlash from these setbacks.

Nevertheless, the rest of the trip exceeded all expectations. When the train pulled into Glasgow's Bridge Street station guns were fired in salute. It was the biggest tourist party the city had ever seen and they were led by a brass band to a reception in the City Hall.

The next stop was Edinburgh. As in Glasgow, the party's arrival met

Above: *Loch Lomond*

with great excitement. Once again they were welcomed at the station by a band which then escorted them through the streets. In the excursionists' honour a special musical event had been arranged for them in the evening by the renowned publisher and temperance advocate William Chambers.

From Edinburgh the tour continued to locations of particular interest, one of which was Loch Lomond. The party enjoyed sailing on this beautiful lake in the midst of stunning scenery. How satisfying this must have been for Thomas. His vision on the summit of Snowdon had now been realised.

Financial collapse

But then he was landed a devastating blow. Despite the overwhelming success of the greater part of the trip, some of his party were still furious because of the lack of conveniences on the journey from Leicester to Fleetwood and the cold, wet, night they had to endure on the deck of the steamer. They decided to take legal action against him.

Thomas had already incurred heavy losses in subsidising his temperance publications and now the costs of these lawsuits aggravated his already fragile financial position. He fell heavily into debt. It was an extremely painful period for him but somehow, in a very short space of time, he managed to come to an agreement with his creditors and narrowly avoided the embarrassment of bankruptcy.

Pressing on

Undeterred by this disturbing experience, Thomas pressed on with plans for further visits to Scotland. In the autumn of 1847 – in an astute marketing move – he organised a tour following a route Queen Victoria and Prince Albert had recently taken to the Highlands and the Hebridean islands of Iona and Staffa. On stretches in remote areas where there were no railway lines, he arranged transport with horse-drawn coaches. Interestingly, the term 'sightseeing' was coined at this time.

When the party arrived on Iona, Thomas was dismayed to see the extreme poverty of the islanders. He was determined to help them. He managed to raise enough money to buy 24 boats fully equipped with nets and tackle to enable them to make a living from fishing. In gratitude to Thomas, the islanders named one of the boats after him. It gave him great joy to have been able to help them and stated:

> *"There is a pleasure in these pursuits which selfishness can never appreciate."*

Sidelined by the railway companies

Just when it seemed that Thomas's tourist business was beginning to take off, the railway companies pulled the plug on him. The reason, quite simply, was that they felt they could run excursions themselves and make a bigger profit by cutting him out as the middle man. It looked as if he was heading for another financial disaster. But ever resourceful, if one avenue was closed to him he looked for another. With rail travel no longer available to him, he concentrated on visits to places of interest within striking distance of Leicester using horse-drawn coaches.

In August 1848 he organised the first of these local trips. It was to the gardens of Melbourne Hall where he had himself once worked. Although Lord Melbourne would not allow the Hall to be opened, the gardens themselves were attraction enough. Most of Melbourne's 2,000 inhabitants turned out to witness the unusual spectacle of a brass band accompanying a procession of coaches carrying over 100 visitors through their village.

This excursion was followed by a visit to Belvoir Castle, home of the Duke of Rutland. Lord Rutland recognized that Thomas was trying to break down the barriers between different classes by making travel affordable to all and wrote to him,

"I fully concur with you in the desire which you express to see the different classes of our great community bound together by ties of increasing strength."

Six horse-drawn coaches took the excursionists to Belvoir Castle and such was the excitement that music was played at each village they passed through along the 28-mile route from Leicester.

The next stately residence to open its doors was Chatsworth House, the grand home of the Duke of Devonshire. The party was given a warm welcome by the Duke himself and to add to their enjoyment he proudly displayed his various collections.

The booming Scottish market

Thomas had found a ready market for his coach trips to local places of interest but in an unexpected change of heart the railway companies asked him to resume his services for them. They had found they just couldn't manage without him.

With the railways once again at his disposal, Thomas escorted two parties to Scotland in 1849 totalling about a thousand people. He also organised tours to North Wales,

Above: Scottish tourist handbook

Ireland, the Isle of Man and Blackpool. By 1850 he had escorted over 15,000 passengers some 7,500 miles and was able to add 'Excursion Agent' to his advertised list of business activities.

He saw the Scottish market as the key to the phenomenal growth of his business and wrote that Scotland *"almost imperceptibly, transformed me from a cheap excursion conductor to a tourist organiser and manager."*

For all but one year between 1848 and 1863 he organised four annual excursions there, taking as many as 5,000 people each season. Fired with enthusiasm he now turned his mind to wider horizons:

> "By the end of the season of 1850 I had become so thoroughly imbued with the tourist spirit that I began to contemplate foreign trips, including the Continent of Europe, the United States, and the Eastern Lands of the Bible."

The Crystal Palace and a national reputation

Intending to make America his first foreign destination, Thomas set off for Liverpool to explore the possibilities of trans-Atlantic tourist travel. On the way he stopped in Derby and happened to meet John Ellis, chairman of the Midland Railway, and Joseph Paxton, a director of the railway and also the Head Gardener at Chatsworth. Thomas knew Ellis from excursion arrangements he had made with him in the past and he had met Paxton at Chatsworth House when he organised trips there.

Above: Albert Memorial, London

They told him that Queen Victoria's husband, Prince Albert, was organising the world's first international Trade Fair in Hyde Park, London, to give Britain and the rest of the world the opportunity to showcase their manufacturing achievements in a spirit of peace and friendship. Paxton had been commissioned to design the biggest glass structure in the world to house the exhibits. He had already established a reputation for building a greenhouse at Chatsworth – the Great Conservatory – which at the time was the world's largest glass building.

Thomas applauded Prince Albert's idea and the spirit behind it. As a central aim of all his excursions was to bring *"man nearer to man"* he promptly agreed to Ellis and Paxton's request to suspend his American plans and organize rail excursions from the Midlands and the North to the Fair instead.

To ensure that low-paid manual workers should be able to visit the Exhibition *"not as to a show or place of amusement but a great School of Science, of Art, of Industry, of Peace and Universal Brotherhood!"* Thomas arranged cheap fares for them, even though it meant a big reduction in his own profits.

The Great Exhibition, as the Fair was called, was opened by Queen Victoria on 1 May 1851. Paxton's impressive glass structure became known as 'The Crystal Palace' and attracted six million visitors during the Exhibition months May to October.

With the help of his son John, now seventeen, Thomas transported 150,000 excursionists to London and back during the Exhibition months. Travel was mostly through the night but

Left: Joseph Paxton

some excursionists were not keen to spend the night on the train so Thomas arranged accommodation for them in London. But there was no such luxury for himself. He rarely spent a night at home, sleeping instead on the floor of the trains.

The Great Exhibition was a significant landmark in Thomas's career in the travel business. His careful planning and organisation ensured that the trips ran very smoothly and earned him national recognition as an excursion organiser.

First tour abroad

Following the success of the Crystal Palace trips,

Above: *The Crystal Palace*　　　　**Inset:** *The plaque at the former entrance*

Thomas led expeditions to other major exhibitions. He also organised circular tours in Ireland and Scotland. With the income he had earned from these ventures he built new premises in 1853 at 123 Granby Street, Leicester, which served as a temperance hotel, his home and his business HQ. He also set up a soup kitchen for the poor

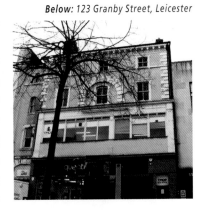

there. Next door he built a temperance hall providing wholesome entertainment such as concerts, sketches and readings.

By 1854 his tourist work had become so time-consuming that he decided to devote himself wholly to it and give up his printing business. He was now 45.

A year later he felt ready to cross the English Channel for the first time and escorted a party of 25 to Brussels and Paris, continuing with them on a Rhine cruise from Cologne to Strasbourg. He repeated this a month later with a group of 50.

Although neither tour was a commercial success, they met with the warm approval of the participants. After the first tour Thomas was presented with a testimonial of thanks by the party and given permission to quote their praise in his company magazine. His *"Christian manner"* had deeply impressed them. He had left no stone unturned in his care for them and in his meticulous attention to detail in making the tour so enjoyable.

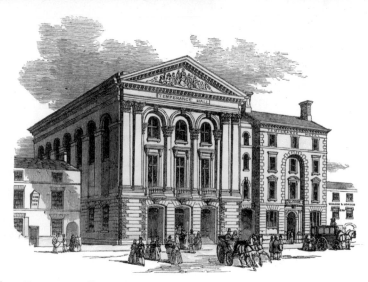

Above: Temperance Hall & Hotel, Leicester

The tour also inspired a deep appreciation of the beauties of nature. One young woman wrote in her diary,

"the glorious sights that have filled my mind with such ideas of natural beauty, have also in some degree, purified and refined my thoughts and given me higher concepts of the Creator."

This was precisely the effect Thomas had hoped for. He stated that one of his main aims in taking parties abroad was to give as many as possible the opportunity *"to behold the handiwork of the Great Supreme"* and thus bring people closer to God.

Another setback overcome: the glories of Switzerland
Despite the positive response of the tourists, Thomas suspended his trips abroad for a few years and concentrated on his Scottish

tours. By 1860 some 50,000 people had travelled with him there but two years later this door suddenly closed. Remarkably, as had happened before, the Scottish railway companies decided to replace him with their own personnel to increase their profits. It was a calamitous blow. Without Scotland Thomas's business could not survive. Once again, his resilience and resourcefulness overcame any inclination to despair and he now turned his attention to Switzerland.

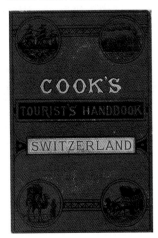

He planned a tour that would present the breathtaking grandeur of the Alps at their best and on 26 June 1863 more than 130 tourists set off with him to Paris, 62 of whom continued with him by rail to Geneva. From there he accompanied some of the party to Chamonix and Martigny, all framed by magnificent Alpine peaks. This tour was a massive success and others followed in rapid succession.

In the summer of 1864, in another dramatic about-turn, the Scottish railway companies realised they couldn't manage without Thomas's expertise and invited him to return to their fold. But this time he declined. He had successfully replaced his Scottish business with Continental tours and these fully occupied him. In fact, they were so popular that he began to cast his net ever wider. On 4 July 1864 he set off on his first tour of Italy visiting Rome, Naples, Pompeii and Mount Vesuvius with a party of over 90. The success of this tour resulted in a very quick repeat.

"God's earth is for the people"
Thomas was enjoying huge success but profit was never his main motive. He had much higher ideals. When outlining his plans for one of his Italian trips, he made it clear that

> *"any who can not accompany us in a genial, sociable and confiding spirit will be kind enough not to join our parties. ... We have been accustomed to look upon our work in the character of a mission of goodwill and universal brotherhood."*

He was convinced that foreign travel could break down distrust between nations and believed that if people of different nationalities actually met each other they would discover that they shared a common humanity. This, he argued, would encourage peace and remove the constant threat of war.

Thomas always insisted that his excursions fostered *"enlargement to mind and deepening of charity"* and wrote:

> *"It is delightful to see, as we travel on, the breaking down of partition walls of prejudice ... the expansion of the intellect ... the benevolent sympathies excited by a more extended knowledge of the circumstances and sufferings of fellow creatures".*

He also observed that *"Christian ministers of various creeds and churches have thrown off the asperities of sectarianism and have sung, prayed and fraternized together in many exercises of devotion, praise and charity."*

But his noble aims triggered fierce opposition. Not for the first time he became the target of ridicule and contempt. He offended people who believed that he was encouraging the wrong type of person to travel to locations that should remain the exclusive preserve of the upper class. His tourists were scathingly dismissed as *"low bred"*, *"stupid"*, *"a mob"*, *"Cook's Circus"* and *"Cook's Hordes"*. How could they possibly appreciate the wonders of nature or the glories of art and architecture?

Despite the fact that his tourists were impeccably well-behaved and appreciative of all that they saw, prejudice against them persisted. Thomas was infuriated by the arrogant attitude of snobs who wanted to *"reserve statue and mountain, painting and lake, historical association and natural beauty for the so-called upper classes"*. He made his position perfectly clear to them:

"I see no sin in introducing natural and artistic wonders to all" and stressed that *"God's earth with all its fullness and beauty is for the people"*.

Above: Naples brochure

To America

But no amount of criticism could hold him back. Having opened up Europe he decided to visit America to explore its potential as a tourist destination, a realistic possibility with the ending of the American Civil War in 1865. Furthermore, he now had sufficient time as he had confidently entrusted his son John with the full-time administration of the business at the company's new headquarters in London which had opened that year in Fleet Street. John was a dynamic character who, in addition to his administrative responsibilities, travelled some 50,000 miles annually consolidating existing markets and opening up new ones. In recognition of his substantial contribution to the business he was eventually made a full partner in 1872 when the company's name was changed to Thomas Cook and Son.

Thomas set off for America on 29 November 1865 sailing from Liverpool to New York. From there he started an exploratory tour of both the USA and Canada to gauge their market

Above: Cook's American Tours

potential. He spent eleven weeks away travelling some 4,000 miles by rail. His journey took in Philadelphia, *"the great Quaker city"* where he spent a *"marvellously quiet"* Sunday; Washington DC; Springfield, Illinois, where he visited the home and tomb of Abraham Lincoln who had been assassinated a few months earlier; Chicago; the spectacular Niagara Falls; and Montreal. It was an indication of his priorities that he wrote home to Marianne to tell her about the deep impression a service at a Baptist chapel in New York City had made on him.

In the spring of 1866, just two months after Thomas's return, John led a tour following his father's trail. Although no further tours took place on that continent for seven years, John eventually established America as a popular tourist destination.

Above: John Mason Cook

The Holy Land – "The greatest event of my tourist life"

As a devout Christian Thomas had long felt drawn to the Holy Land *"to trace out sites and scenes immortalized in the Bible"*. At the end of 1868 he made an exploratory trip to Egypt and Palestine (modern-day Israel) to assess their viability as tourist destinations.

It was a courageous step. He had been warned that there were no railways or proper roads in Palestine and that coach travel there was impossible. There was also the ever-present threat of robbery. In fact, those who knew that region advised travellers to go armed and with an escort. This would be no trip for the faint-hearted.

Undeterred by these drawbacks, Thomas assembled an intrepid party of 32 who left London on 24 January 1869 for a 105 day tour of Egypt and the Holy Land. After crossing the Mediterranean from Brindisi to Alexandria, the party continued their journey by rail to

Cairo where two steamers were hired to take them up the Nile to Giza to visit the Pyramids and the Sphinx and then to Luxor to explore the Valley of the Kings. After a truly memorable stay in Egypt, the party set off for Palestine and the gruelling part of their tour.

After the sea crossing from Alexandria to Beirut, the hardy tourists endured up to eight hours a day on horseback, then spending the night in tents. They made their way through difficult, hot, dusty terrain to some of the most familiar-sounding locations in the Bible – Bethlehem, Jericho, the River Jordan, the Dead Sea and of course, Jerusalem.

As expected, not everything went well. While camping outside the walls of Jerusalem the party was robbed and a considerable amount of money stolen. However, the culprits were quickly apprehended and compelled to repay the stolen money. In addition, one of the thieves was ordered by the authorities to hand over a house he owned in Bethlehem to Thomas who unhesitatingly donated it to The Society for the Promotion of Christianity Among the Jews, one of the many missions he supported. The Middle Eastern tour, despite its difficulties and discomforts, made a deep impression on the party. They were well aware that Thomas had smoothed their path as much as humanly possible and in

Above: Palestine and Egypt Tours

gratitude to him for his care and attention they signed a testimonial in recognition of the *"honourable, efficient and straightforward manner in which he has fulfilled his engagements"*.

Above: Cook's tourists in Egypt

For Thomas this was much more than a trip to a distant country – it was a pilgrimage. He afterwards told the *Leicester Journal* that it was *"the greatest event of my tourist life"*.

Enthused by the success of the tour, Thomas organised more, ever conscious of their spiritual benefits. Looking back after four years of leading visits to the Holy Land, he wrote with considerable pleasure:

> *"the educational and social results of these four years of Eastern travel have been most encouraging. A new incentive to scriptural investigation has been created and fostered"*.

He went on to establish *Biblical, Educational and General Tours for Ministers, Sunday school teachers and others engaged in promoting scriptural education.*

By 1891, the company's 50th anniversary, some 12,000 pilgrims had used his services to travel to the Middle East. Among them were leading members of European royalty, including the future King of England, George V. The mockers who had disparaged Cook's tourists as *"low bred"* and *"a mob"* had to eat their words.

First round-the-world tour

Thomas's next great challenge was to circle the globe. He had attended the opening ceremony of the Suez Canal on 16 November 1869, the 102-mile canal which made it possible for ships to travel between Europe and India by connecting the Mediterranean Sea and the Red Sea. The previous route had been around Africa, 4,300 miles longer. This phenomenal work of engineering opened up new and exciting possibilities for Thomas and he began planning the first ever leisure tour round the world.

On 26 September 1872, now 63, he set off from Liverpool for New York with nine companions. It was a 25,000-mile journey that would take 222 days. The party travelled from New York across the USA to San Francisco, stopping off en route to see, among much else, Niagara Falls, Chicago, the Rocky Mountains and Denver. From San Francisco they sailed across the Pacific to visit Japan and China. During the stay in India, Thomas was deeply moved by the visit to Serampore where his hero the renowned missionary William Carey had served. The Taj Mahal in Agra was another highlight of his stay in that country. From India the party returned to England via the Red Sea and the Suez Canal.

Such was the interest in Thomas's journey that *The Times* invited him to send regular reports for publication in the paper. Ever mindful of his Christian priorities he also sent reports to two Baptist newspapers. As he explained to readers:

"In a tour around the world, missions and missionaries constitute natural topics of thought and of conversation; indeed, I regard this subject as one of the elements of special interest to engage the attention of travellers. … On board the steamers of the Pacific and these Eastern seas, we are almost certain to meet with missionaries travelling to and from their fields of labour."

It is hardly surprising that Thomas, a former evangelist, should be so passionate about the work the missionaries were doing. He was clearly inspired by those he met on his travels, writing:

"the missionary subject has presented itself to me with renewed and increased force, and I felt as though I could not but speak and write of the things I have seen and heard."

He was convinced that his missionary reports *"will be appreciated by many who laudably contribute to the support of Missionary operations, and who labour and pray for the conversion of the world to Christ."*

On his journey Thomas met two people who made a particularly deep impression on him. One was Rev. James Smith who ran a mission station in Delhi. This clergyman was so highly esteemed that he was invited to give an address to Prince Alfred, the Duke of Edinburgh (Queen Victoria's second son) when the Prince visited Delhi. Thomas was inspired by Smith and praised him in the following way:

"*I question if in Delhi there is a man more respected or who yields a more potent influence for good than the Rev. James Smith ... with all he says his great and only teaching is to make Christ known as the only Saviour. I could not but feel how puny many revilers of Christian missions would look in the presence of such a man.*"

He was also struck by the "*constant readiness for missionary work*" of a Mrs. Ward on board the steamer. He was impressed by "*her daily and careful teaching of one of our Chinese waiters who had learnt to read the Scriptures in San Francisco and desired a more perfect knowledge of the way to salvation, that he might be able to teach his fellow countrymen on his return to China.*"

Thomas himself took advantage of any opportunity that arose on the journey to share his faith. In Chicago he gave a sermon at the Freewill Baptist Chapel and while in Benares, India, he was "*invited to the Baptist Sunday School, where I spoke words of encouragement to about seventy children and a number of actively devoted teachers*"

This first round-the-world leisure tour so captured the

imagination of the public that it became an annual event. By the time of Thomas's death in 1892 almost 2,000 people had circumnavigated the globe with his company, a tremendous tribute to his visionary thinking and pioneering spirit.

Rift between father and son
The same year Thomas completed his global tour, 1873, business was booming and the company opened new purpose-built headquarters in Ludgate Circus, London. John was put in charge of operations there. The company's continual growth should have been a source of great satisfaction to both father and son who, on the outside, might have seemed to form the perfect team. But, sadly, this was not the case. They had totally opposite attitudes to business and a gulf opened up between them that grew ever wider.

John was uncompromisingly profit-driven and it infuriated him that his father did not appear to treat business seriously enough, always giving priority to his religious and philanthropic activities. He was frustrated that Thomas devoted so much time and money supporting missions around the world and visiting them as often as he could. He also fiercely objected when Thomas gave concessionary fares to Baptist parties travelling to Rome in 1875 and the United States in 1877. Thomas's joy that *"the social feeling has risen above the commercial"* was something that John simply could not understand.

Writing to Marianne on 24 March 1873 from one of his tours to the Holy Land, Thomas gave his account of the rift between himself and their son:

"He does not like my mixing Missions with business but he cannot deprive me of the pleasure I have in the combination; it has sweetened my journey and I hope improved my heart without prejudice to the mercenary object of the tour. I shall neither be expelled from the office nor stifled in my spirit's utterance, and I have told him so very plainly."

John was equally as direct about their business relationship: *"we never worked well together and … our notions of business were so opposite that I did not believe we ever could."*

But his patience finally ran out. In a letter to Thomas on 22 February 1878 he wrote:

"I state distinctly that I will not sign nor enter into any new arrangements for partnership with you upon any terms; all your recent letters prove the impossibility of us working together. … I .. refer you to my repeated offers commencing at least three years back when I asked you to relieve me of a partnership which had always been irksome to me".

With the partnership agreement due to expire on 30 December 1878 John made it clear he would not renew it. On 8 August he wrote to Thomas: *"I must be left unfettered as the sole manager"* and insisted that he should have *"sole legal and monetary responsibility"*. Thomas, now 70, had just built 'Thorncroft', a house on Leicester's London Road for his retirement and John no doubt felt that his father no longer had his mind fully on the business anyway. And so, early in 1879, the partnership was dissolved *"by mutual consent"* and John took full control of the company.

Despite the tension between them, they clearly felt some degree of affection and respect for each other. Thomas was always open to reconciliation and had written to Marianne "*I know my heart is right towards him.*" Long

Above: Thorncroft

after the partnership with John had ended, Thomas signed a letter to him *"Your truly affectionate father"*.

John, too, however sharp the content of his letters to his father, always signed them *"Your affectionate son"*. He also recognized that his father's vision and pioneering spirit had laid the foundations on which the success of the company had been built and his respect for Thomas was clearly evident when he graciously wrote to him at the time their partnership ended:

"As long as you live I want you to have half the profits of this business."

The tragic death of Annie

With no further involvement in the company, Thomas moved into his retirement home in Leicester with Marianne and their daughter Annie. He immersed himself in church and temperance work, becoming more actively involved in the Archdeacon Lane Baptist Chapel where the family had worshipped since the time they had first come to Leicester. Annie was a dedicated teacher

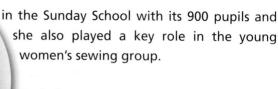

in the Sunday School with its 900 pupils and she also played a key role in the young women's sewing group.

Sadly, just two years into Thomas's retirement, the family was struck by tragedy. On Saturday 6 November 1880 Annie, aged 35, was overcome by fumes from a faulty gas water-heater and drowned in her bath at home.

Above: Annie Cook

Thomas and Marianne had been very close to Annie and were inconsolable at her death. Thomas lost little time in deciding how to honour her memory. Annie herself had drawn his attention to a piece of land opposite Archdeacon Lane Chapel which she felt would be ideal to erect a building for the Sunday School. Only a week after her funeral a letter from him was published in *The Leicester Chronicle* stating his intention to do just that. The Annie Cook Memorial Hall and Sunday School Room were duly opened less than two years later on 30 April 1882. Among other things in his speech, Thomas stated that the Hall would be for general hire but would not be let for *"any object which was avowedly hostile to the principles of the Christian religion"*. Both alcohol and smoking would also be forbidden.

Marianne never got over Annie's death and in the course of the next three and a half years her own health gradually declined. Thomas took her to various spa and seaside resorts but these had no effect. Her last year, Thomas wrote, was one of *"extreme trial"* and on the 8 March 1884 she died, aged 77. She was laid to rest with Annie in Leicester's Welford Road Cemetery.

The death and legacy of Thomas Cook

After the loss of Marianne, loneliness was a heavy cross for Thomas to bear. However, he found great strength in his faith and he took particular comfort from his favourite hymn *Forever with the Lord.* The words in that hymn *"Be Thou at my right hand,/Then can I never fail;/Uphold Thou me, and I shall stand,/Fight, and I must prevail."* were no doubt a source of great encouragement to him.

Despite his bereavements, Thomas remained positive and active. Even after turning 80, when he became increasingly frail and blind, he continued to attend temperance meetings and travel and when he was completely blind he actually travelled to the Holy Land. His last public act was to unveil a block of almshouses and a mission hall in 1891 in his home village of Melbourne in memory of his beloved wife and daughter. In addition to the loving bond he had enjoyed with them, they had faithfully supported him in all his business activities and frequently accompanied him on his excursions. Annie, a fluent French speaker, often acted as his interpreter.

Above: Almshouses and Mission Hall, Melbourne

But eventually his frailty caught up with him and when the end came, it came out of the blue. About 8 p.m. on 18 July 1892 he was having supper at home when he suddenly felt unwell with a severe pain in his side. The doctor was called but could do nothing to help. Three hours later Thomas, aged 83, was dead. He had suffered a fatal stroke.

The Archdeacon Lane Baptist Chapel was full to overflowing for his funeral service. The hearse carrying his coffin was pulled to Leicester's Welford Road Cemetery by six black horses bedecked with plumes of black feathers. They were followed by the Mayor of Leicester at the head of a procession of twelve horse-drawn carriages. Flags in Leicester were flown at half-mast. In the cemetery itself a great crowd was present when Thomas was laid to rest with Marianne and Annie.

In its obituary the *Leicester Daily Post* quoted the praise expressed for Thomas the previous year by William Gladstone, four times British Prime Minister, when the company celebrated

Above: Archdeacon Lane Baptist Chapel

its 50th anniversary:

"Thousands and thousands of the inhabitants of these islands who never would for a moment have passed beyond its shores, have been able to go and return in safety and comfort, and with great enjoyment, great refreshment and great improvement to themselves."

Even before then Gladstone had observed that through Cook's tours *"whole classes have, for the first time, found easy access to foreign countries, and have acquired some of that familiarity with them which breeds not contempt but kindness."*

It would have given Thomas great joy to know that his tours had helped bring *"man nearer to man"*. He would also have been delighted that he had helped bring man *"nearer to his*

Above: *Thomas Cook statue, Leicester*

Creator" by making accessible *"God's earth with all its fullness and beauty"* to countless millions. It is easy to understand, therefore, why William Gladstone esteemed him so highly and ranked him among the nation's great *"public benefactors"*. Like Gladstone, we can all admire Thomas Cook for his remarkable achievements and we can be grateful to him for the wonderful gift of affordable leisure travel he gave to the world.

Acknowledgements

The following have given me invaluable help with my research. I am most grateful to them.

Rev. Nicholas Cook, *Minister, Market Harborough Baptist Church*

Jess Jenkins, *Archivist, Record Office for Leicestershire, Leicester and Rutland, Wigston Magna*

Alison Mott, *Loughborough History and Heritage Network, Loughborough University*

Ian Porter, *Loughborough Library Local Studies*

Gillian Pritchard, *Loughborough Library Local Studies*

Paul Smith, *Company Archivist, Thomas Cook UK & Ireland*

Douglas Wooldridge, *Archivist, Market Harborough Baptist Church;*

also Archivist, East Midland Baptist Association, Nottingham

Images

Thomas Cook Archives have very kindly given permission to use the following:

Thomas Cook (p 1)

Marianne mason (p 7)

Handbook of the trip to Liverpool (p 18)

Scottish tourist handbook (p 25)

Temperance Hall & Hotel, Leicester (p 30)

Tourist's handbook, Switzerland (p 31)

Naples brochure (p 33)

Cook's American Tours (p 34)

John Mason Cook (p 35)

Palestine and Egypt Tours (p 36)

Cook's tourists in Egypt (p 37)

Cook's tours round the world (p 40)

Annie Cook (p 44)

Thanks are also due to:

British Listed Buildings – Market Harborough Town Hall (p 10)

Carley Evangelical Baptist Church – Joseph Winks (p 5)

Alan Murray-Rust – Baptist Chapel, Borrowden (p7). No change has been made to the original.